Andrea Cremonesi and Marco Degl'Innoce

Meet Sebastian
VETTEL

THE STORY OF FORMULA ONE'S
YOUNGEST CHAMPION

To all my fans.

SOUVENIR
PRESS

PRAISE FOR SEBASTIAN VETTEL

"He won 18 out of 20 races during his first experience with
the Red Bull Junior Team. This not only proves his talent,
it demonstrates his great commitment as well. He pursues
technical perfection in every way, and he expects his team to
do the same. His constant efforts to nurture these qualities
made him the outstanding driver he is now".

Dr. Helmut Marko, former F1 driver and Mateschitz's collaborator

"He's a fast driver, he's fun, and he's a jolly fellow.
He has a brilliant future ahead, and working with him
is a real pleasure".

Christian Horner, Red Bull Racing Team Principal

HIS TEAM DESCRIBES HIM AS...

"A German with a British sense of humour".

"One of us...".

"The fastest German driver ever – besides,
he's even funnier than Michael...".

"Exceptionally fast...".

"A phenomenal driver, endowed with
an incredible team spirit".

"Young and full of enthusiasm".

"He even loves Monty Python!".

"He is one of the most interesting emerging talents
who entered the F1 world during the last decade. Being a
fast racer is not his only asset: his outstanding capacity to
build meaningful relationships is remarkable too, because
it allows him to get the best from his team".

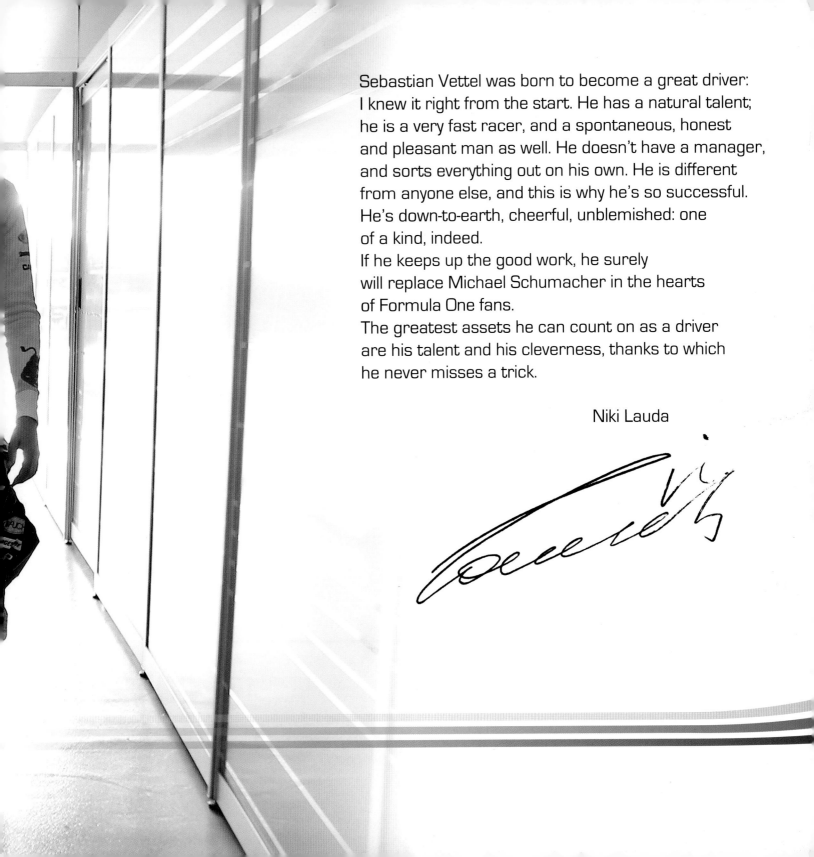

Sebastian Vettel was born to become a great driver:
I knew it right from the start. He has a natural talent;
he is a very fast racer, and a spontaneous, honest
and pleasant man as well. He doesn't have a manager,
and sorts everything out on his own. He is different
from anyone else, and this is why he's so successful.
He's down-to-earth, cheerful, unblemished: one
of a kind, indeed.
If he keeps up the good work, he surely
will replace Michael Schumacher in the hearts
of Formula One fans.
The greatest assets he can count on as a driver
are his talent and his cleverness, thanks to which
he never misses a trick.

Niki Lauda

The first time I saw him drive,
I told myself: "This boy is going
to be a world champion".
He's extraordinarily talented,
he's a lovely young man,
he's fast and competitive:
he has everything it takes to
become a Formula One champion.

Bernie Ecclestone

Bernie

INTERVIEW

IN HIS OWN WORDS

Question: When exactly did you start thinking about becoming a world-class driver?

Answer: "It must have been when I started taking part in F1 competitions: before then, racing was nothing more than a leisure activity for me. However, participating in world-class races is not enough to be considered a real driver: what matters most is to earn the public's respect, regardless of your level and your success".

Q: Do you remember the first Grand Prix you ever saw?

A: "My father was a F1 enthusiast. I remember watching Senna win a Brazilian Prix; I was still a little child back then".

Q: This is a particularly thriving time for motor racing in your country: can you explain why?

A: "I don't know, it probably has to do with the smooth organisation that characterises our system at all levels".

Q: Do you live in a house or in a flat?

A: "I have a country house, a sort of farm, not far from Zurich Airport. Living within easy reach of planes is vital to my job".

Q: You are said to be very curious, and keen on having eventful holidays.

A: "Lying in the sun for two weeks is not for me. Last year, after the world championship, I travelled to America, rented a car and spent my holidays driving around. I even drove to Scandinavia, once".

On opposite page, Sebastian Vettel is interviewed by Andrea Cremonesi. Below, Sebastian Vettel (right) poses with Michael Schumacher.

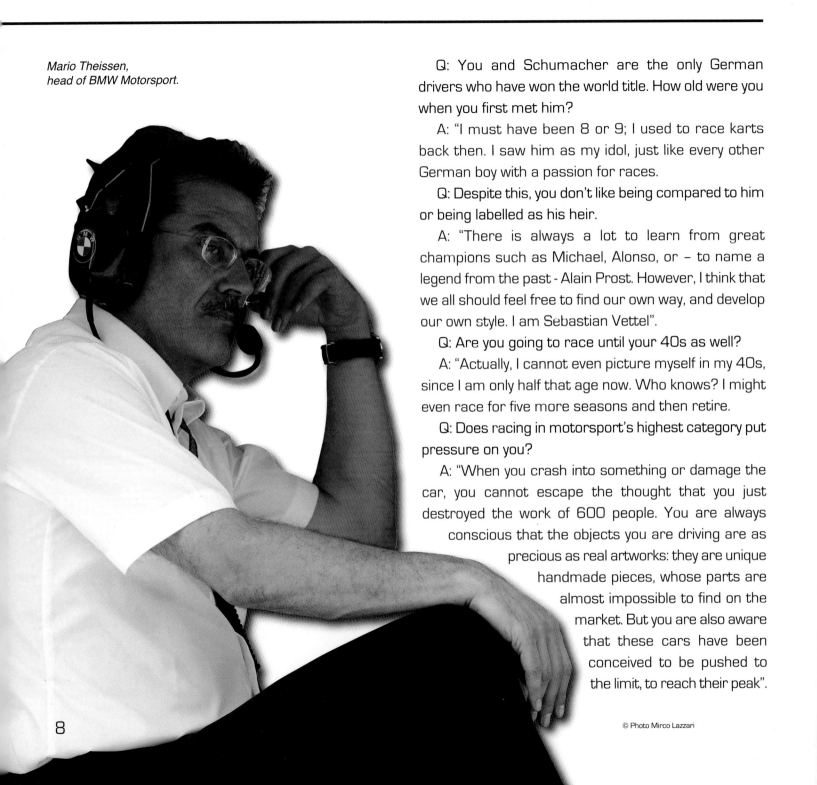

Mario Theissen,
head of BMW Motorsport.

Q: You and Schumacher are the only German drivers who have won the world title. How old were you when you first met him?

A: "I must have been 8 or 9; I used to race karts back then. I saw him as my idol, just like every other German boy with a passion for races.

Q: Despite this, you don't like being compared to him or being labelled as his heir.

A: "There is always a lot to learn from great champions such as Michael, Alonso, or – to name a legend from the past - Alain Prost. However, I think that we all should feel free to find our own way, and develop our own style. I am Sebastian Vettel".

Q: Are you going to race until your 40s as well?

A: "Actually, I cannot even picture myself in my 40s, since I am only half that age now. Who knows? I might even race for five more seasons and then retire.

Q: Does racing in motorsport's highest category put pressure on you?

A: "When you crash into something or damage the car, you cannot escape the thought that you just destroyed the work of 600 people. You are always conscious that the objects you are driving are as precious as real artworks: they are unique handmade pieces, whose parts are almost impossible to find on the market. But you are also aware that these cars have been conceived to be pushed to the limit, to reach their peak".

Q: Do you still feel excited when you are behind the wheel?

A: "I have been racing for so long, that I know perfectly well what it feels like. Before starting a race, I prefer to stay away from people: I don't talk to anyone, I concentrate on my tasks. I also listen to music".

Q: What kind of music?

A: "Melodic music makes me relax. It's better not to listen to Lady Gaga in moments like those".

Q: Is it true that you are a Beatles fan?

A: "I have been a Beatles fan ever since my childhood when I started to appreciate music. My parents used to listen to them, and their songs are still special to me".

Q: How would you define your relationship with your family?

A: "Our bond is very strong. They attend as many GPs as they can, and if they can't make it in person we talk a lot on the phone. My father and I are very close: he was my mechanic when I raced karts and could not afford to pay someone to fix my accidents. He has always been free with advice, and helped me a lot. Generally speaking, I have always seen my family as my point of reference, especially during hard times".

Q: You have a younger brother, too.

A: "I do. He's 12, and would like to start racing as well, but our father prefers to tread carefully as far as this aspect is concerned".

Q: Did your parents sacrifice for you?

A: "Of course they did. For example, we used to spend holidays at kart tracks, sleeping in a camper van,

Dr. Helmut Marko, operational assistant for Dietrich Mateschitz, also known as Mr Red Bull.

© Photo Mirco Lazzari

instead of going on ski trips."

Q: You always have a smile on your face; do you ever get angry?

A: "Of course: I even shout, when something goes awry. However, I always try not to disrespect the people who work with me. After all, we are all here to improve our performances; it would be absurd to always smile and say 'OK, no problem, everything's going great'".

Q: Is it difficult to speak the truth in F1?

A: "Yes, it is. It's often better not to speak your mind at all. It's not a matter of personality: you always have to keep in mind that this isn't just a sport, it's also a huge business that encompasses many different interests".

Q: Speaking of business, why don't you have a manager?

A: "When I was younger I was involved in the Red Bull programme, and therefore I was managed by Dr. Helmut Marko; then I entered BMW, and Mario Theissen began to look after my interests. A manager shouldn't simply walk around with a briefcase and claim a right on a part of your earnings: he should be absolutely trustworthy, someone to believe in. I still haven't found such a person, and I never even felt the need to look for one: I always managed everything with my family".

Q: Are there any choices that you regret?

A: "Not for the moment. What really matters, is to know what you want. I only had problems once, when I made my debut with Toro Rosso, because I missed my

flight. In the end, however, I still reached the racetrack on time".

Q: Do you have any friends in F1?

A: "At present I don't have any. Kimi Raikkonen was my friend in F1, but he left for other projects".

Q: How do you feel towards the car you drive? You are known for giving her nicknames.

A: "It's quite a different kind of relationship, comparing to the ones you build with human beings. Still, you have to live in symbiosis with your car. You have to treat it like you would treat a pretty girl, be kind to her, respect her; otherwise, it will leave you stranded".

Q: What makes the difference between a good driver and a champion?

A: "Your mind. And the amount of self-confidence you have".

Sebastian trains on a kart.

Q: Do you like to be on your own?

A: "Taking a break from F1 from time to time would probably do me good, but I cannot really manage to do it. Before heading to Mount Vesuvius, I had faced the much more demanding challenge of climbing Mount Fuji, after the 2008 GP. I love wandering on the mountains; what I enjoy most is reaching the top, looking down, and relishing the peak I have climbed".

Q: Apart from hiking, what other sports do you like?

A: "A lot of them, really, even if I admit I'm not a great curling fan...! Actually, I think that every sport can teach you a lesson worth learning. For instance, speaking about motorcycling, I'm a great fan of Valentino Rossi".

Q: You are still at the very beginning of your career in F1; which results do you consider as your greatest achievements so far?

A: "My first victory ever, in Monza, and my first victory with Red Bull Racing in China".

Q: What about your hardest time?

A: "It happened in Brazil, in 2009, when I realised that my pursuit of the world title was over. We all knew that winning it would have been hard, but me and the guys really believed that it was possible. However, we retired in five races during that season, which was too much: winning the championship requires absolute constancy".

Q: How did you feel when you were awarded the world title?

A: I felt I was going through an amazing experience: winning the world title is the dream that all drivers

© Foto Express

Vettel drives his Toro Rosso in Faenza (2009).

cherish ever since their childhood, and I had just made it come true. It all happened during the last race...what a great feeling! The number 1 on my car makes me feel proud, but it makes me think about my responsibilities as well: I'm now well aware that I am Formula One's ambassador.

11

How do you feel about racing at Silverstone?
"I would say that it's the only country where it rains and it's sunny at the same time. The track is really great and I know that all the drivers enjoy racing here. It has some fast corners where you really have to have guts. I really love coming here and it is kind of a home race for us."

So, it is important to the team?
"It's a nice race and it means a lot to us, as it's the home Grand Prix for the team, being so close to here. Probably you have a lot of teams which it's their home Grand Prix, and it's special to all of us. It's the same as every weekend: We try to do our best, and try to beat the other one. Nothing changes just because of the fact we are in Silverstone."

How do you like the renovation of Silverstone?
"It's true that the buildings are very modern and we all have a lot of space to work in so that's a good aspect. I think it's a bit sad that the fans coming here can hardly see the pit stops as there is quite a significant difference between the level of the track and that of the grandstands. And, for us drivers, it's a bit sad that we have lost the first corner because I

Vettel and athletic trainer Tommi Parmakoski climb Mount Vesuvius (2010).
On the right, Sebastian's celebrations after his pole position and winning in Monza (2008).

think that Copse was always something special. When you were standing at the pit wall you could see how quickly the cars were flying towards you and then they turn right. Well, that's now a thing of the past, but if you only look backwards you don't make a single move forwards."

Do you feel after every victory that it will be harder to win at the next race?
"Who said that it was ever easy to win? And the 'Vettel finger' only goes up when we really deliver the maximum. I know some here don't like it, for obvious reasons, but I must say that it was never my intention to bruise someone's ego with it. But there is the danger that you start to feel too comfortable in your role as the leader of the pack. It is key that you concentrate on every little bit so you reach the target. You shouldn't stare at the target as then you stumble over the little steps."

Sebastian's views on Silverstone are taken
from an interview conducted with the Formula 1 website

© Photo Mirco Lazzari

Let's rewind, now, and go back to 15 years ago. We will head to Kerpen, to the kart track where a certain Michael Schumacher cut his teeth.

*Sebastian Vettel with Andrea Cremonesi (right)
and Marco Degl'Innocenti at the Red Bull Energy Station
(the team's reception room during GPs).*

THE ROOTS OF A GREAT PASSION

Young Vettel's destiny was determined one day in 1995. It couldn't have happened anywhere but there, at the most famous kart track ever: Kerpen - Manheim, Germany, the cradle of Michael and Ralf Schumacher.

Sebastian's father, Norbert, had read the papers, and found that the track was going to host a very important race: the Land Nordrhein-Westfalen Cup. Only 34 participants were allowed to take part in the children's race; however, much to his and Sebastian's surprise, over one hundred contestants had applied for the qualifying round. All of them were there to impress Michael Schumacher, who had already been racing with Ferrari for three years, and had been the event's patron for quite a long time already.

Shortly before the beginning of the final round, rain started to fall. All contestants had slick tyres, and many of them started replacing them with rain tyres. When little Vettel – definitely the youngest and smallest there – was approached by Michael Schumacher, he asked him if it was possible to keep the slick tyres on despite the weather: "it is possible, but it's not easy at all", answered his idol. Sebastian pushed hard on the accelerator right from the start of the race, defending

1996: Almost unrecognisable, young Vettel proudly poses near his idol Schumacher, after winning the NRW Cup on the Erftlandring Kerpen - Manheim track.

his lead until the last lap, when he was overtaken by another driver: in the end, he came second, and was awarded a cup and Michael Schumacher's congratulations. Curiously enough, during the whole race he had been sitting on one of Schumacher's caps: "It was a coincidence" – he recalls – "the cap was on my seat, and I didn't even notice it until I left the kart. It might have been my lucky charm...who knows?"

Great Schumi, who had already won two world titles at that time, had no doubts about the future of the young driver he had just shaken hands with: "this boy will surely become a champion". But he couldn't have imagined that the boy would have taken his first steps in F1 shortly before his own retirement, and that one day he would have become a formidable challenger to him on the racetracks.

Nowadays, Sebastian Vettel is continuously being compared to Michael Schumacher: in Germany, he has already been labelled as his heir. Indeed, they both are very talented drivers; besides, however different they might sound, their personal lives share many common features as well.

Sebastian Vettel grew up in a simple family – still wealthier than Schumacher's, whose father Rolf worked as guardian at Kerpen kart track, and whose mother Elisabeth cooked fritters at the track's refreshments kiosk. However, both drivers come from the German provinces. Kerpen, with 30,000 inhabitants, is near Cologne; Heppenheim, where Sebastian was born on 3 July 1987, is a small town, populated by little more than 25,000 people, and located 60 km south of Frankfurt – not far from Hockenheim racetrack.

Sebastian's father, Norbert, is 52-years-old and owns a small interior furnishings firm. When he was young, he used to race in a Golf GTI that he took care of in his own garage at home. It was Norbert who offered Sebastian his first kart when he was three.

During the summer holidays, the whole family enjoyed renting mini-karts in the tourist resorts they visited. "I decided to buy one as well", says Norbert. "The one I chose had a small 60cc engine, with just 3 CV horsepower, and transmission on just one wheel.

The kart was actually a Christmas present for Sebastian's older sisters, Stefanie and Melanie. Both the girls were quite good at driving it; nevertheless they soon had to find another pastime. In fact, Sebastian started chalking up one lap after another in the courtyard at the age of only three and a half and rapidly monopolised the kart. Seppi – as he is known within his family – categorically refused to let go of it, or share it with his sisters.

The improvised track he drove on was marked off with old car tyres; to make more challenging, Norbert used to soak it with bucketfuls of water. His son learnt very quickly how to handle curves and control the drift. "I just wanted to share my passion with my children, and to keep them away from the streets", Mr Vettel recalls.

At the age of seven, Sebastian already had his licence to drive karts; however, it was only after his eighth birthday that he could take part in his first race. It took place close to home, on the Waldorf track, near Heidelberg; Sebastian was the youngest contender, and came third.

As soon as he realised that Seppi really had a way with karts, Norbert started to watch races with him every weekend. "We travelled together in the family station wagon". Sometimes, they even attended "real" F1 races.

Sebastian's first experience with the great champions' cars happened, of course, on the nearby Hockenheim racetrack. His father had bought tickets for the German Grand Prix practices: standing places, on the lawn, in front of an unimpressive chicane. "It was raining, we have been standing in the mud for hours." – Sebastian recalls – "Sometimes a car passed by, but it disappeared immediately". Nevertheless, that day his destiny appeared to him clearer than it had ever been: sooner or later, he would drive one of those single-seats as well.

"Being a close family has always been very important to us", points out Norbert. Before heading to the tracks where Seppi was racing, Sebastian's mother, Heike, used to prepare refreshments for everyone. Stefanie, 28, a physiotherapist for children with special needs, was their timekeeper: she could record timings

Sebastian, in his teens, sits behind the wheel of a Formula BMW-ADAC and talks to Gerhard Berger, director of BMW Motorsport at that time (Norisring racetrack, 2003).

19

for six drivers at the same time with a simple manual chronograph. Besides Stefanie and Melanie, 26, a dental technician, the family fan club counts another member: Fabian, 12, who is still going to school.

Over time, after Sebastian had started racing in single-seats, the station wagon was replaced by a camper van; the camper van then became a comfortable motorhome, in which the Vettels still follow their beloved driver to most European racetracks. The elder sisters live in the family home, but they both work and are very busy; despite this, and Fabian's commitment to school, they still manage to travel together sometimes.

Sebastian himself successfully finished his education. In 2006, apart from making his debut in the F1 world, he received his Abitur and left school. Sebastian attended the prestigious Starkenburg School in Heppenheim: "The completion of his studies was a very important matter, both for us and for him." – his father points out – "He was the first to recognise that racing does not guarantee a secure future. He was a normal student, a fast learner who didn't need to spend too much time over books. Luckily, he didn't have any classes on Saturdays; however, sometimes he had to miss school on Fridays – of course, with the teachers' and our consent. When he entered Formula BMW we spoke to the headmaster, and she said 'It's not a big deal if he misses classes, as long as he has a private tutor that helps him catch up'. We followed her suggestion, and it worked well. His school agreed to support him, as long as he didn't neglect his studies too much".

Of course, Sebastian attended another kind of class as well: as soon as he turned 18, he obtained a driving licence. However, there was very little left for him to learn: "It was him who taught me how to face the curves on our mountain roads", recalls instructor Herald Meyer.

However, his first experience on a car was not thrilling at all. It took place in the family courtyard, in a Ford Fiesta, when Sebastian was only 13: Norbert wanted to teach him how to combine the accelerator and the clutch as this does not exist in kart racing. The route he had to follow was slightly uphill, and Sebastian could only drive a few metres before scratching the car's flank on a tree. "He was completely unfamiliar with the dimensions of a real car", recalls Norbert, quite amused. "He was too used to sitting in the middle of a kart…he was so clumsy while riding the car, with the driver's seat on the left".

Matthias Wilkes, Bergstrasse district's councillor, is proud of his famous fellow citizen as well: "It is clear that such a successful Formula One driver is also a valuable testimonial for our area, which boasts an exceptional quality of life. However, it must not be forgotten that Harald zu Hausen, Nobel Prize for medicine, was born in Heppenheim as well. Anyway, what I like most about Sebastian is his open-mindedness, which he has maintained despite his success".

Brisighella 2009.
On the left, Matthias Wilkes, President of the Heppenheim Province; in the middle, Cesare Sangiorgi, Mayor of Brisighella, with Sebastian Vettel.

NOACK, THE TALENT HUNTER

Q: When did you first meet Sebastian Vettel, and on what occasion?

A: I met him in 1995; he was 8. He came to my track, in Kerpen, to race in the children's league.

Q: What impressed you most about him?

A: All of a sudden, it started raining very hard. He was using smooth tyres, and he dealt with the difficult conditions more brilliantly than everyone else: I found this greatly impressive, considering his very young age. That particular race made Sebastian stand out in my eyes.

Q: How did your collaboration with Sebastian begin, and how long did it last?

A: I appreciated Sebastian for three main reasons. First of all, because he was a good kart driver; secondly, because he had an innate tendency to drive fast; thirdly, because he was a very friendly boy – very polite, as well, unlike many others. As had happened with Michael Schumacher, I felt a strong desire to help him. I started to look for patrons, and Red Bull was one of the most influential sponsors I found; nevertheless, I also had many other backers, without whose help we would never have been able to progress as Red Bull had granted us a very small budget at the beginning. For this reason, I'm still very grateful to everyone who supported us. I'm not driven by profit: I'm happy when a driver who started his career with me makes it to Formula One. It's something that makes me proud, the biggest reward I can hope for my work.

Q: Did you follow Sebastian only while he was driving karts, or did you support him also when he switched to single-seats?

A: I followed his experience in Formula ADAC – BMW as well. And, as a friend, I'm always there to give him advice.

Q: Did you recognise right from the start that he had the potential to become a F1 world champion?

A: I have been sure about it since the first time I met him. Sebastian is the kind of person who starts working before the rest of the team in the morning, and finishes after everyone else has left. He was always curious about all the technical issues, and always able to provide first-hand information about what needed to be improved. Such an attitude is what characterises a potential champion; Sebastian has been showing it even when he was still driving karts.

Gerhard Noack
in his team's motorhome.

23

Q: Did you immediately think that he was on his way to become the new Michael Schumacher?

A: Yes, because Sebastian showed all the characteristics that made Michael unique: resilience, fighting spirit, pride, and a fierce will to always be the best, together with an insatiable appetite for victory.

Q: What is the difference between Sebastian and Schumi, both as drivers and as individuals?

A: It's a too personal question; I would like to keep the answer to myself.

Q: What is Sebastian's best asset?

A: His personality. Not only does he act nicely and pleasantly in public: he is nice and pleasant. And he has a peculiar sense of humour as well. This is why everybody likes him so much.

Q: Does he have any flaws as well?

A: Not that I know – but, even if he did, I would prefer not to reveal them: our bond is still too strong for this.

Q: How would you define your current relationship?

A: We are both very busy with our jobs so we cannot devote much time to each other, but we are still in touch via text and e-mail. He invites me to his F1 races, and in winter he often races on my track in Kerpen; on these occasions we talk a lot. But I'm not disappointed that he has so little spare time: it means that he's having a lot of success.

Vettel with Schumi, (still racing for Ferrari at that time), and Noack.

25

PASSIONS AND SUPERSTITIONS

Sebastian doesn't show up very often in the town where he was born – where an Italian restaurant, La Dolce Vita, offers a dish called "Spaghetti Vettel". At the beginning of his career with BMW-Sauber, he actually moved to Walchwil, a Swiss village of 3,000 inhabitants; later on, he moved into his new residence between Zurich and Lake Constance.

Nevertheless, Vettel always goes back home on the holy days: he never fails to spend Christmas with his family, singing along to the traditional carols that his mother Heike insists on repeating every year. In reality, Sebastian has never liked to sing, but this doesn't mean that he dislikes music. He is particularly keen on rock music from the '60s and the '70s, and he's a passionate Beatles fan: he owns a record-breaking collection of their original records.

During his first year with Red Bull, he could fulfil one of his most cherished dreams: at an auction, in England, he bought an extremely rare album, With The Beatles, which contains the original autographs of the Liverpool quartet. It cost him £2,700 at the time.

There is a peculiar anecdote about this purchase: the previous owner of that record was Ann Bradshaw, a very popular figure in the F1 world, who had worked as Williams' and BMW's press officer for a very long time. Bradshaw, who had won the record at a prize draw organised by an English newspaper in 1963, auctioned it in order to earn the money she needed to refurbish her bathroom!

As soon as he learnt the news, Vettel sent her a text from Suzuka (where he was taking part in the Japanese Grand Prix), asking her to attend the auction

and buy the record again on his behalf. "Many people were interested in it, and the price was rising very quickly." – says Ann Bradshaw – "The last bidder gave up when it reached £2,600, and I could finally outbid him".

Ann Bradshaw gave Vettel the rare vinyl at the last race of the season in Abu Dhabi.

Another of Vettel's favourite pastimes is exploiting his talent as a mimic. He particularly likes to impersonate German celebrities: his favourite target is former football player and national team manager Franz Beckenbauer, a giant of German sport. His family and friends, and the people at Red Bull, scream with laughter when Sebastian performs his best acts.

Sebastian Vettel is superstitious as well: nothing strange, considering that he's a F1 driver. Those who know him well swear that he changes direction every time he sees a black cat cross the road, going blocks out of his way to avoid it. Moreover, as with many other drivers, he also has his own talismans: one of them is a pig-shaped charm he received from his father, who bought it at a petrol station where they had stopped to refuel the camper van after an unsuccessful kart race. "Take it: you'll see, the next race will be alright", said Norbert with a smile.

More recently, Sebastian started carrying with him a coin and a small medal, which he slips in his suit or shoes during the races. He found the coin – an American cent – while he was jogging in a park, in 2007, on the eve of his first F1 race in Indianapolis. The other lucky charm is a small medal with the image of Saint Christopher, patron saint of motorists; his grandmother, Margarete, brought it back from a pilgrimage to Lourdes.

Another of his quirks is calling the F1 cars he drives women's names. "Calling racing cars with feminine names is an English tradition, which applies to ships as well." – he explains – "My first Toro Rosso was called Julia. The name of my first Red Bull was Kate; I crashed it while racing against Kubica in Australia. We had to change the body shell, so Kate was promptly replaced by Kate's Dirty Sister". Sebastian laughs, remembering that the English word "dirty" can assume a different meaning in Italian: "in this case, the most suitable synonym is 'aggressive'".

Translating the name of the RB6 he drove in 2010 was tricky as well: in fact, it was called "Luscious Liz". But Liz proved not to be luscious at all: after his team-mate Webber won in Monaco, Sebastian claimed his car was not fast enough, and therefore obtained a new chassis. Of course, he didn't forget to give a name to the car he drove during the following Turkish GP: he called her "Randy Mandy". Unfortunately, it didn't bring him any luck: during a failed attempt to overtake Webber, who was leading the race, Sebastian collided with him, went off the road, and had to retire from the competition. The single-seat he used in 2011 was called "Kinky Kylie", as a tribute to Australian pop star Kylie Minogue. Red Bull's boss Dietrich Mateschitz has now offered it to him as a special present, to reward him for the achievement of his second World Title; the previous year he had done the same, offering Sebastian the car he had driven during the 2010 season.

February 2010. Vettel climbs snowy Mount Vesuvius (1281 meters)
with athletic trainer Tommi Parmakoski.
Naples and its Gulf are visible in the background.

On top of Mount Vesuvius, Vettel looks at an image of the Virgin Mary on lavic rock.

32

*A souvenir of the excursion
on Mount Vesuvius
(1281 meters).*

On the Hawaiian shore, Sebastian Vettel runs with a surfboard in hand, during one of Red Bull's international promotional campaigns. America is one of the destinations that drivers appreciate most, because they can wander around undisturbed.

34

Time's up: it's 6am, and Sebastian Vettel heads back
to the Hawaiian shore to avoid running into awakening sharks.

Vettel as a footballer: he plays with Nazionale Piloti as a left midfielder. His shirt carries the number 37. He is also a fan of Eintracht Frankfurt, a team in the German Bundesliga.

© Photo Angelo Scaroni

*Politecnico di Milano, 2009:
Vettel gives a lecture with
engineer Geoffrey Willis,
Red Bull Racing's Technical
Director at that time.*

41

*Vettel and Willis,
during their lecture in Milan.*

*Outside the Polytechnic, Sebastian poses
with a group of students.*

Vettel at the gym.

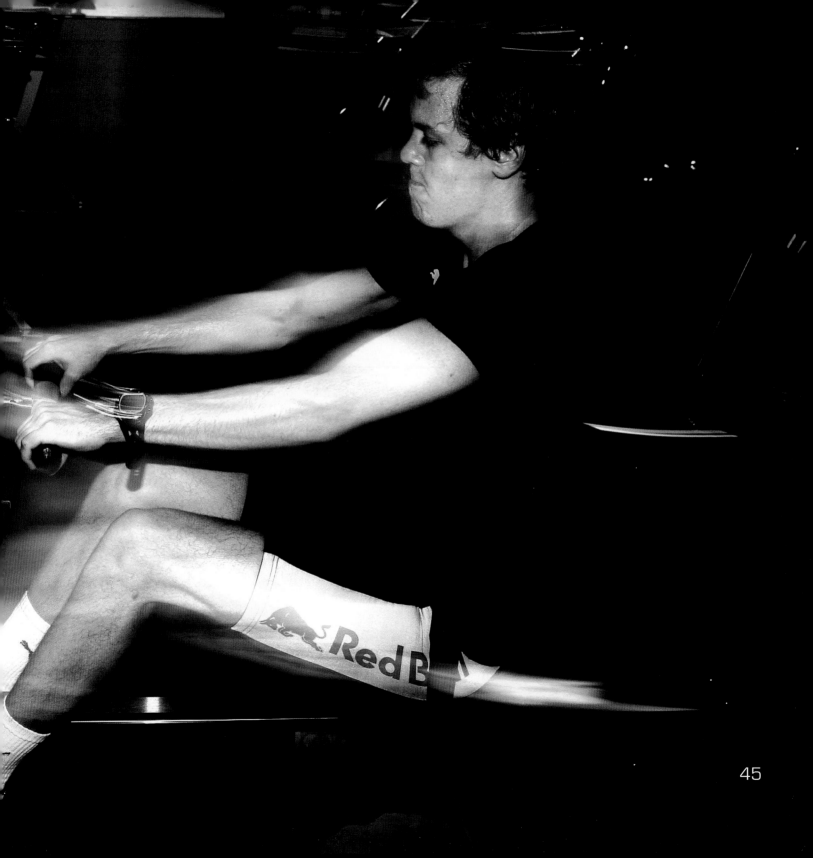

VETTEL

TONY//KART

Vettel drives a kart from the Italian stable Tony, based in Brescia.

Monza, August 2008: sitting on an old Vespa, Sebastian Vettel admires the beautiful Villa Reale.
Less than one month later, Monza became the theatre of his first success in a F1 GP.
The following was shot by German television station RTL.

*Monza: Vettel poses in front of the Cathedral,
and then, again, at the Villa Reale.*

© Photo GN Motorsport

FROM KARTS TO F1

In Kerpen, young Vettel was immediately spotted by Schumi's first mentor, Gerhard Noack. Noack offered him a place in his team, and gave him financial assistance as well: he was of great help to Norbert Vettel, who recalls "The first kart season was not that expensive, we spent only 7,000 Marks. Later on, however, I had to sell my own racing car, and I quit races to devote my time to my son. We wouldn't be here if it hadn't been for Noack: he gave us financial support, he found the sponsors, and he launched Sebastian in the racing world". Until then, the family had to make many sacrifices. In order to support his grandson's rising racing career, Grandpa Werner had sold his farm. Sebastian's father, Norbert, had even mounted an additional tank on the family station wagon: this way, he could drive to Italy – where Sebastian used to travel quite frequently for kart races – without having to stop off in Switzerland, where the price of fuel was higher than in Germany. Sometimes, Seb himself had to sleep on a blanket in the car trunk, so that his parents could avoid spending money on a hotel room.

After his experience with karts – which led him to win the title of Junior European Champion in 2001 - Sebastian entered Formula BMW – ADAC in 2003,

Noack's KSN Racing kart team (1997).
Vettel is the first on the right, in the front row.

and started driving 140cv single-seats. By the end of the first season, he was second in the final rankings; the following year he won the Championship, with 18 victories out of 20 races – a record that still stands.

The Munich-based stable immediately took him under its wing, and so did Dietrich Mateschitz, Red Bull's patron. Despite the former partnership, that ended despite a promising start, Sebastian's relationship with the world famous brand that "gives you wings" never failed; as a matter of fact, it was crucial for his success in F1.

After spending two seasons in F3 Euroseries – with a total of four victories during the second year, and the achievement of coming second overall – and two successes in World Series Renault, Sebastian joined F1 as test-driver for BMW – Sauber in 2006. On the 25th of August, the team asked him to replace Polish driver Kubica during the Friday practices, as Kubica had just been appointed to the first team after the dismissal of the disappointing Jacques Villeneuve; at that time, Sebastian's experience on a single-seat amounted to less than 500km.

"What a strange feeling. I will compete with my idol Michael Schumacher, we will be racing on the same track: what if I set a faster time? Such things happen, sometimes, during Friday practices", said the young German driver, unflappable while the media besieged

Frank Lucke, Team Mücke's Racing Engineer,
bends over Sebastian's Formula BMW – ADAC (2003).

Sebastian Vettel

him with questions. No sooner said than done: on the Istanbul track - which he had only had the chance to study on a simulator - he set the fastest time, seven tenths of a second ahead of Michael Schumacher's Ferrari, which came only seventh. Still, he was punished for his rampant enthusiasm: after a radar trap caught him running 4 km/h beyond the speed limit in the pit lane he had to pay a $1,000 fine.

He performed even better on September 8th, during the practices for the Italian GP: he set the fastest time in both the trial sessions.

On the left, Sebastian stands on the podium in Nürburgring, wearing a funny costume; below, Sebastian overtakes the Brazilian driver Atila de Abreu, in Zandvoort. On the right, Vettel standing on his car (Zandvoort, Netherlands, 2004).

Sebastian Vettel drives the training car that BMW and ADAC (German Automobile Club) promoted in Hockenheim (2-3 October 2004). The "Smileys" on the passenger compartment keep score of his victories in Championship races.

"Baby Schumi" – as everybody had started to call him – had his big day on 16 June 2007. At the age of 19, 11 months and 14 days, he was the sixth youngest driver to debut in a Formula One race – and, what's more, on a legendary track: Indianapolis.

"You will race in Sunday's race", announced Mario Theissen, Team Principal at BMW – Sauber, the previous Thursday afternoon. The Polish driver, Robert Kubica, had been in a frightening but harmless accident during the Canadian GP and had been pronounced as unable to race by the FIA doctors. Vettel immediately called Germany to give the good news to his parents, and started focusing on his debut. He finished eighth and he became the youngest F1 driver to score in a race.

19 September 2004: Vettel wins race 2 in Brno (Czech Republic), and the Formula BMW – ADAC League. In the photo below, he celebrates with the team.

© BMW Motorsport

Vettel's joy after winning at Nürburgring (1 August 2004).

After Indianapolis he returned to his usual job, and waited for another opportunity to race in F1: to those who asked him how he saw his future, he replied that "drivers don't like to sit and wait". As far as it seemed, BMW was growing cold towards him: Kubica regained his place as soon as he recovered from the accident, while German driver Nick Heidfeld, who had still not won a race, was considered irreplaceable by the team.

Nevertheless, the Red Bull family was ready to give Sebastian a warm welcome. Sister stable Toro Rosso, based in Faenza, was looking forward to getting rid of Scott Speed, and finally dismissed the American racer without notice. At the time, Toro Rosso was jointly owned by former Ferrari driver Gerhard Berger and industrialist Mateschitz, building on the foundations established by the Minardi team.

Michael Schumacher himself contacted Berger

Below, Sebastian laughs with Mario Theissen
and Bernie Ecclestone (Turkey, 2006).
On the right, proud Vettel holds his FIA Super Licence.

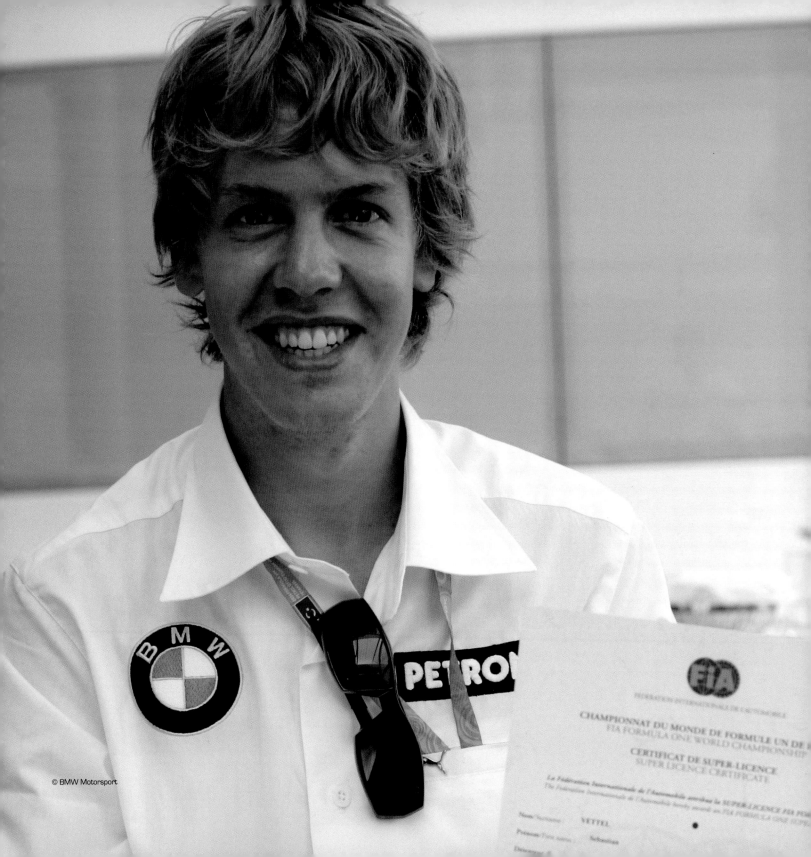

Sebastian Vettel drives his Toro Rosso in the rain (Fuji, 2007).

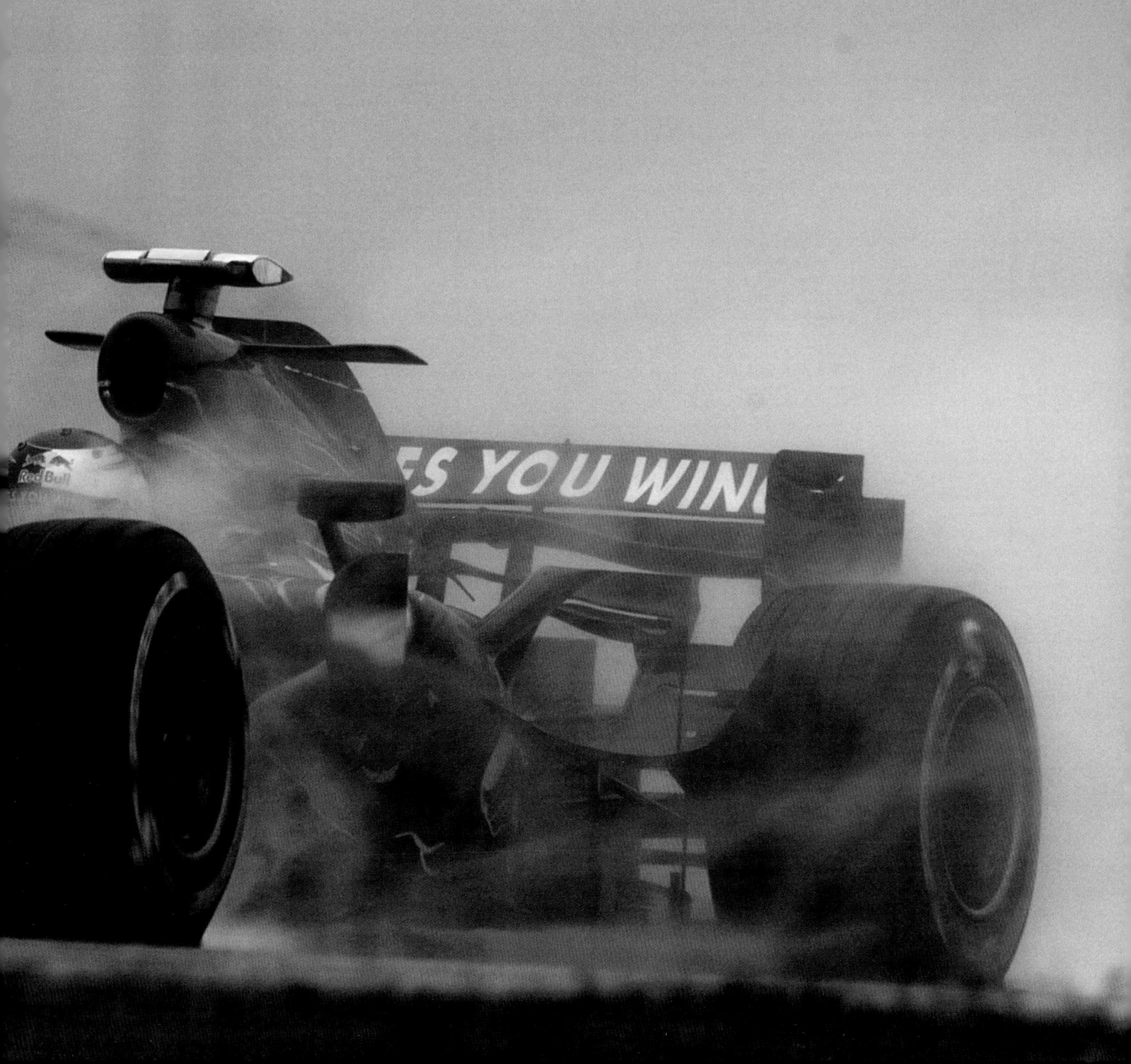
ES YOU WIN
Red Bull

from the Maldives, where he was spending his holidays, advising him to hire Vettel: "We all want him to become a top-class driver", declared the Austrian manager, while announcing Vettel's entry into Toro Rosso. Sebastian made his debut at the Hungarian GP, together with Italian racer Vitantonio Liuzzi. He finished in a mediocre sixteenth place, reflecting the difficulty of dealing with a new car for the first time.

The price he had to pay at the Japanese Grand Prix, which took place in Fuji in the pouring rain, was way higher and much more painful. During the 45th lap, he crashed into Red Bull Racing's Mark Webber, who went off the track; before the accident, the Australian driver was in second place, while Sebastian was third. The disappointment was so great that he burst into tears; in hindsight, it almost prefigures what would happen three years later in Turkey.

At the end of the season, BMW was still unable to decide what to do with Vettel; such indecision lasted for too long, until the option that entitled the Munich-based

stable to call him back from Toro Rosso finally expired. Later on, Mario Theissen admitted that some of the top managers were not convinced that the young German driver was mature enough to race with BMW. On the other hand, Dietrich Mateschitz's team – and especially his right-hand man, Helmut Marko – strongly believed in Sebastian, to the point that they asked him to stay with Toro Rosso for one more year. The first races of 2008 didn't live up to the expectations: Vettel's inexperience resulted in a series of accidents, which forced him to retire from three races out of five. He scored his first points in Monaco, where he came fifth. The race in Valencia marked his turning point, leading to a series of good performances that reached its climax in Monza.

On the left, Robert Kubica's terrible accident in Montreal (2007): it forced him to miss the United States Grand Prix, leading to Vettel's debut in F1. Below, Mark Webber leaves his car after the crash with Vettel in Fuji (2007). On the right, Sebastian Vettel celebrates his success in the British Grand Prix (Silverstone, 2009).

Giorgio Ascanelli,
Toro Rosso's
Technical Director.

"NO ONE BRAKES LIKE HE DOES"

"Sebastian Vettel is an extraordinarily brilliant individual". Such praise comes from Giorgio Ascanelli, born in Ferrara on 3 September 1959, and holder of a prestigious track record in the racing world. He started his long career with Ferrari in 1985; he then worked with Benetton and McLaren, went back to Maranello, and experienced the GT scene with Maserati. Finally, he was offered a place at Toro Rosso by Gerhard Berger, with whom he had previously worked as track engineer. He developed his skills and experience in England and Italy, collaborating with many of the drivers who made their mark in F1 during the '90s: Gerhard Berger himself, but also Nelson Piquet, Ayrton Senna, Jean Alesi and Michael Schumacher.

"I was greatly impressed by Vettel's attitude after his debut in Hungary, because he dared to admit openly that he had made a mistake. It's not often that drivers recognise their faults: many of them prefer to justify themselves with weak excuses. The fact that Vettel was willing to challenge himself is proof of his fortitude".

Q: In what ways did he improve himself over the past few years?

A: "Sebastian has always been a fast racer, but at the beginning he lacked the awareness of why he could drive so fast - which is what really makes a great driver. It took him time to figure it out, but I am proud to say that he has finally become a mature driver".

Q: In your opinion, what was the race that marked the turning point in his career?

A: "Valencia, in 2008: he set the fastest time despite racing with used tyres and having the car weighed down by the fuel in the tank. His unstoppable ascent started back then".

Q: Which leads us to his victory in Monza, one month later.

A: "The previous Saturday afternoon we had a meeting to define the strategic aspects of that GP. We knew that, even if Sebastian raced at his best, reaching anything higher than third place (or second, perhaps, with a bit of luck) would have been improbable on a dry track. "Let's hope for the rain!", I added. After the race, I told him "enjoy this moment, because nothing feels as good as your first victory". That day went down in history: before Sebastian's performance, the last victory by an Italian car that was not a Ferrari dated back to 1957, when Juan Manuel Fangio won the German GP".

Q: Apart from his cleverness, what are Sebastian's most remarkable qualities?

A: "His capacity to remain focussed, his ability to concentrate on only one thing at a time, his personal driving style and the use he makes of tyres. But what strikes me most is that no one brakes like he does".

Q: What do you mean?
A: "It's a secret, and it's better not to reveal it to his competitors...".
Q: How would you define Sebastian?
A: "A destroyer. As far as this aspect is concerned, he's a true German. He works hard, leaving nothing to chance. He's one of the

2008: Under the eyes of Gerhard Berger, Vettel shakes hands with Schumi, who was working as a consultant for Ferrari at that time.

©GEPA pictures/Franz Pammer

best active drivers, taking his chances against Alonso and Hamilton".

Q: Does he remind you of any of the F1 champions of the past?

A: "I really can't tell. When I met Senna, he had already become world champion more than once. When Sebastian met me, he was so in awe that he called me Sir!".

Dietrich Mateschitz, Red Bull's boss, congratulates Vettel after his excellent performance in Monza (2008).

© GEPA pictures/Andreas Reichart

Sebastian celebrates his victory
in Monza with the Toro Rosso team.

75

THE FIRST SUCCESS

Monza was suffering from terrible weather on 14 September 2008; such bad conditions were quite unusual given the area and the time of year. The Autodromo Nazionale has been hosting the Italian GP since its opening in 1922; the competition always takes place during the first half of September because in Brianza late summer is usually characterised by sunny days and dry weather. However, that particular morning Sebastian Vettel woke up to heavy rain. His dream of winning that day's race – the dream he shared with the whole Toro Rosso team, born in 2006 after the fall of Minardi - had begun 24 hours earlier, when he gained his first pole position in F1. When he saw the livid sky outside his window he felt that making it come true was within his grasp.

"If it rains, pole position gives me a significant advantage: compared to the other teams I will have better visibility, and my visor will not be steamed by the spray that the other cars will throw up", he told the media the previous afternoon, while the Toro Rosso and Red Bull Racing teams were celebrating his success in qualifying.

Sebastian was only 21 at the time, but he had

Triumph after the victory in the Italian GP (2008).

already established a record: he was the youngest leader of an official qualifying session. Gerhard Berger, head of the Faenza-based stable, already knew that victory was on its way: "He's tomorrow's champion", he predicted.

The hours before the race seemed to be passing with unbearable slowness: in the end, the starting signal came along with a sense of release. Inside the car Sebastian fastened his seat belts, while the mechanics encouraged him: "Go Sebastian, destroy them", they said, playful and serious at the same time.

Vettel burst out laughing, as he had done the day before, when he explained why he thought that his pole position had not been a stroke of luck: "Before heading to Spa, I had stopped by in Kerpen, and tried driving with dry tyres while it was raining. I thought it could be good training for the Belgian GP, but in the end it came in useful here, in Monza. 'I might even reach pole position, if it rains', I told the mechanics before the qualifying round. I was only joking – but see? It happened, in the end".

Sebastian knew the time was right, as his Toro Rosso had already delivered excellent performances on wet tracks. McLaren and Ferrari, the leading competitors for the world title, had both suffered during the qualifying session,... [continues on page 83]

Vettel's Toro Rosso races
in the wet in Monza.

Vettel wins the Italian GP (2008).
At the age of 21 years and 73 days,
he is the youngest driver to ever win an official race.
On the right, the "Gazzetta dello Sport"
celebrates his success.

(continues from page 77)

...because their tyres tended to lose grip on the wet road: Massa – not exactly an ace in poor weather conditions – had placed himself sixth, while Raikkonen and Hamilton, who had already engaged in a no holds barred encounter on Spa's wet track the previous week could not make it past 14th and 15th this time.

At the end of the race Sebastian admitted that the race director's decision to deploy the safety car at the beginning protected him against the problems he might have encountered otherwise. What mattered most to him was not to make any mistakes. "I wasn't even considering that I was leading the race. The track was viscous, I had little grip – I had to be very careful, as a little mistake in braking could have been enough to destroy the work of a whole race".

However, despite his lack of experience, Sebastian did everything right: he was the first to cross the finishing line, after 53 flawless laps, in 1 hour and 26 minutes, at an average speed of 212.039 km/h (which is quite impressive, considering the weather conditions). "This is the best day of my life", he said, while the prize-giving unfolded before his eyes. Drivers love Monza's podium because it leans out above the road, reaching towards the crowd that invades the track after the end of each race (an unfailing tradition since 1970 when Clay Regazzoni won in his Ferrari).

"Driving behind the safety car helped me a lot; later

Monza, 2008: Vettel hugs Gerhard Berger on the podium.

on, I started driving at a good pace myself. But I surely wouldn't have won if it hadn't been for Giorgio Ascanelli. The strategy he outlined was perfect: as I stayed on track longer than Kovalainen, it was easier to assess McLaren's performance on intermediate tyres, and make the right decision when it came to replacing our own tyres. The track started drying out during the final laps, and people at the box kept on telling me "You're first, you're first" – so I thought "Fuck, I can really win". This is such a great joy for me, because I'm very fond of this track. I've loved it since the first time I came here, two years ago. It makes you feel your car is as light as a feather, leaping from one side to another; it's a really special feeling. Winning here, with an Italian car and a Ferrari engine, is a special feeling as well: listening to both the German and the Italian national anthem moved me to tears. Despite being a small team, we proved that we had the balls to win this race, outdistancing Ferrari, McLaren, Renault and BMW".

Besides being the youngest driver to win a F1 GP, Vettel also brought Toro Rosso its first victory, and proved that Ferrari is not the only Italian car that can stand out in official competitions. It had last happened on 4 August 1957, when Juan Manuel Fangio won the German GP on a Maserati 250F, on the way to his fifth (and last) World Title.

Young Sebastian impressed all F1 fans with his enthusiasm and his freshness: in the end, everyone was celebrating as they would have if a Ferrari driver had won, while race director Giorgio Beghella Bartoli offered him the chequered flag that had been waved when he crossed the finishing line. He had never done such a thing before: not even for Michael Schumacher.

GRAN
SANTAN
D'ITALIA

MONZA 2008

THE RISE OF A CHAMPION

Although the title of world champion is still to come, Sebastian Vettel will remember 2009 as the year he made a permanent mark in the F1 world. "We lost the title because we retired from five races, but I still think this has been a great season": he said in Abu Dhabi, explaining what 2009 meant for him, while celebrating his fourth victory of the year and second place in the final ranking. Not a bad result at all, considering that he was only 22 at the time and had never driven a car with such potential before. After the convincing performances Vettel had delivered in 2008, Dietrich Mateschitz and Dr. Helmut Marko had decided to replace David Coulthard and place their trust in him. In the end Sebastian proved them right.

Let's go back to 9 March now. That day, Ferrari's former technical director Ross Brawn started his new career as BrawnGP's manager after rescuing the Brackley plant, which would otherwise have closed after Honda's decision to give up on F1. In Montmelò, where the last test before the beginning of the new season was taking place, he presented his BGP001: the debut was a triumph, as his cars, which didn't even have sponsorship, dominated the test session.

Their distinctive feature was the double diffuser, which bordered on the illegal, and was destined to be the subject of much controversy after the first race. Toyota and Williams had adopted it as well (in fact, it is said that the original idea had been conceived by an engineer who had left one team to work with the other) but only Ross's team had been able to make it work effectively. The season had not yet begun, but BrawnGP seemed to have already defeated its competitors; when races finally started such an impression looked to be certain: BrawnGP's main driver, Jenson Button, won six races out of seven. Only Red Bull Racing could keep up with his pace, until Sebastian Vettel finally managed to take advantage of the British team's only mishap. It happened in Shanghai: Vettel took the second pole position of his career on a dry track, and ran the official race under a rain shower that closely resembled the one he had encountered in Monza. He won, and his team mate, Mark Webber, came second.

Such a result was highly frustrating in a way: if FIA had accepted Ferrari, McLaren, Renault and Red Bull Racing's claims against the double diffuser the first seven races of the season would probably have gone differently as well.

However, motorsport's governing body sided with Ross Brawn, making it difficult for Red Bull Racing to compete with the Brawn's high standards. Adrian Newey's project for RB5 included pull road rear-wheel suspensions, which were quite common in the '90s, as a way to lower the rear carriage. Unfortunately, this meant that there was no more space for a double diffuser, which made it very hard for RB5 to keep up with BGP001.

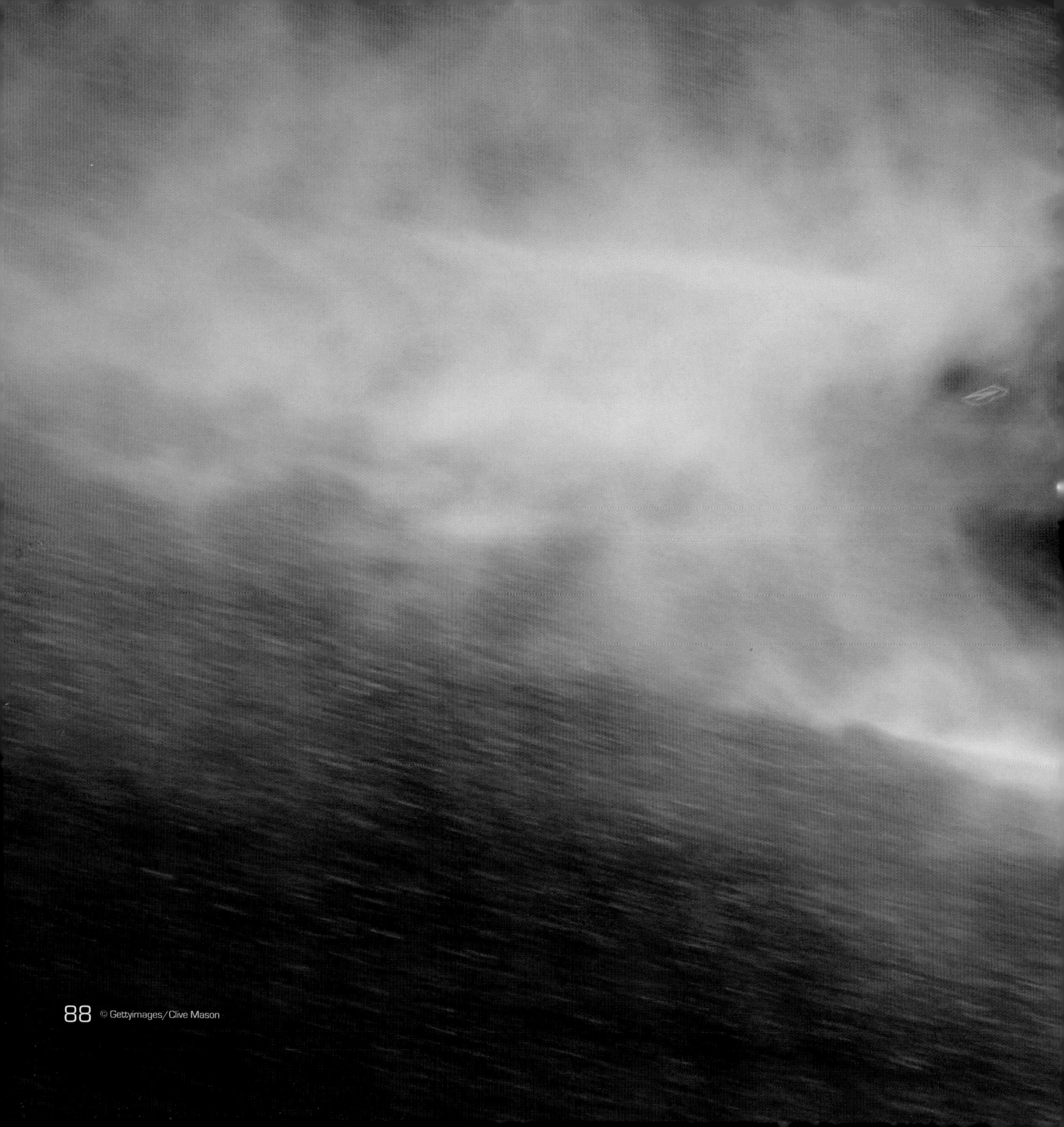

Spa, 2009: journalist Alexander Steudel gives Sebastian Vettel the Sportsman of the Year Award, established by SPORTS BILD, and awarded as a result of readers' votes.

Things started to improve after the Turkish GP. Due to a number of unfortunate choices, and their rivals' constant development, BrawnGP was no longer thought to be unbeatable – even if it could still count on a remarkable advantage, as there was a gap of 32 points between Button and Vettel (61 points against 29), and Red Bull Racing needed 39.5 points to reach the top of the team ranking.

Such gaps were not only due to the technical supremacy of Button and Barrichello's cars: the many mistakes made by Vettel during the first races of the season played a crucial part as well. Sebastian had scored no points in the Australian and Malaysian GPs, because of a crash with Robert Kubica in Melbourne (caused by the German driver himself, while trying to resist Kubica's attempt to overtake him), and a turnoff on the wet track in Sepang. Another accident forced Vettel to withdraw in Monaco; he then won the British GP, starting from pole position, and performing the fastest lap as well: a good omen for the German GP, which was scheduled for three weeks later. However, things went rather differently: to the disappointment of the many fans who had headed to Nürburgring to acclaim their local idol, he lost out to his team-mate, Mark Webber. The Hungarian GP went even worse: despite a good start from the first row, Sebastian had to retire after 29 laps due to a broken suspension. It was an uneasy GP, marked by Felipe Massa's terrible, incredible accident during the qualifying session: an accident that ended the season for the Brazilian driver.

In August, when races restarted after a one-month break, there was no turning point: in Valencia, on a track built by the old harbour that hosts the America's Cup, Vettel was betrayed by his own engine.

The V8 engine was actually the weak spot of the Red Bull Racing cars: regulations prescribe that only 8 different engines can be used during one season, and the team was very close to reaching the limit. This was bad news because the following race would have taken place in Monza where making good use of the engine is crucial.

Vettel was fourth in the world rankings, behind Button, Barrichello and Webber. He needed only 25 points to reach the top: catching up with Button was not impossible, as Jenson, probably paralysed by a sudden fear of losing, had started performing below his usual standards. In any case, Red Bull Racing performed disappointingly in Monza: Vettel and Webber started the race from the fifth row, and Sebastian, on the same track where he had achieved his first success, scored only one point; on the other hand, BrawnGP's drivers came first and second. Still, Vettel didn't think that the challenge was over: "it will be hard to catch up with Button, but this doesn't mean that it's impossible: remember what happened to Hamilton two years ago...", he said, after winning his third race of the season in Japan.

However, the gap between Button and him was considerable: 16 points (85 against 69), with only 20 more points up for grabs in the Brazilian GP and in Abu Dhabi. Sebastian needed a miracle, but the miracle didn't happen: due to the heavy rain that fell during the qualifying session in Interlagos he performed poorly, starting a disappointing 16th on the starting grid. The challenge was over; however, he made such a brilliant recovery in the official race, that he almost made it to the third place on the podium. "If we consider the whole season" – he stated – "Button is certainly the driver who achieved the best results. He deserved the title. Nevertheless, I still think this has been a good year for me".

Brisighella (Ravenna):
On the left, Sebastian receives
the Lorenzo Bandini Prize from
President Tiziano Samorè.

Below, from left to right: former driver Nino Vaccarella,
Mayor Cesare Sangiorgi, Sebastian Vettel, Flaminia Cinque,
Swiss Toro Rosso driver Sebastien Buemi,
Margherita Freddi (Lorenzo Bandini's wife)
and Gabriella Bandini (sister of the late Ferrari driver
who died in 1967 in Monaco).

Vettel in the Premio Bandini 2009 race,
driving the previous year's Toro Rosso.

On the streets of Brisighella.

On the left, Vettel signs Premio Bandini's book of honour.
Behind him stands organiser Franco Asirelli.
Below, another picture with Tiziano Samorè.
On the left, Austrian journalist Tania Bauer can be seen.

*Vettel plunges into
the crowd in Brisighella.
Top left: a picture
with Gerhard Berger.
Below, Vettel talks to the
organisers of Premio Bandini.*

104   © Foto Express

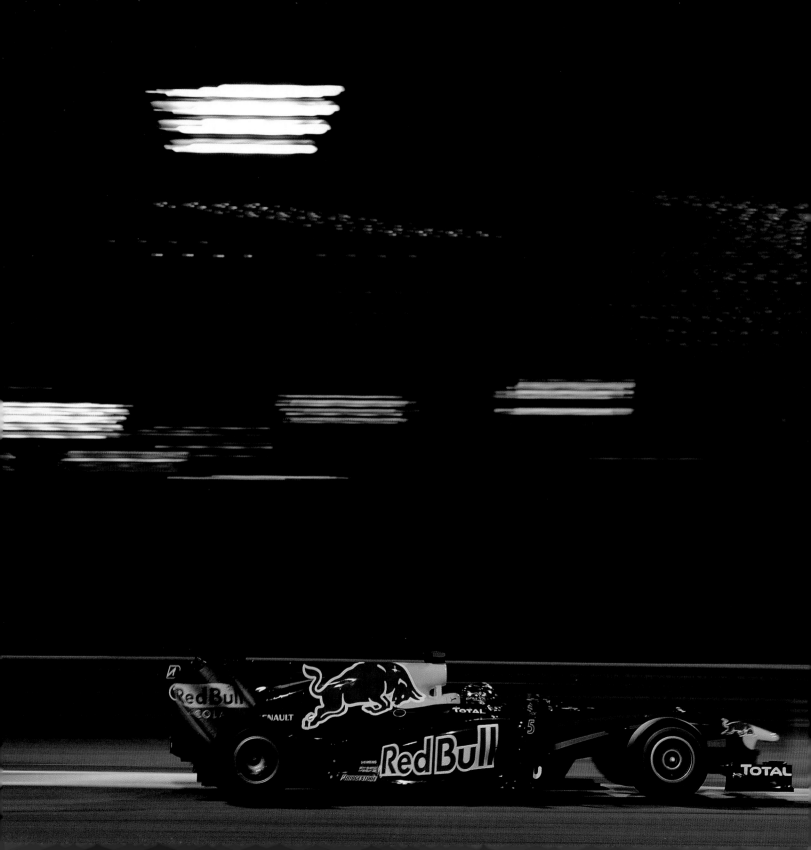

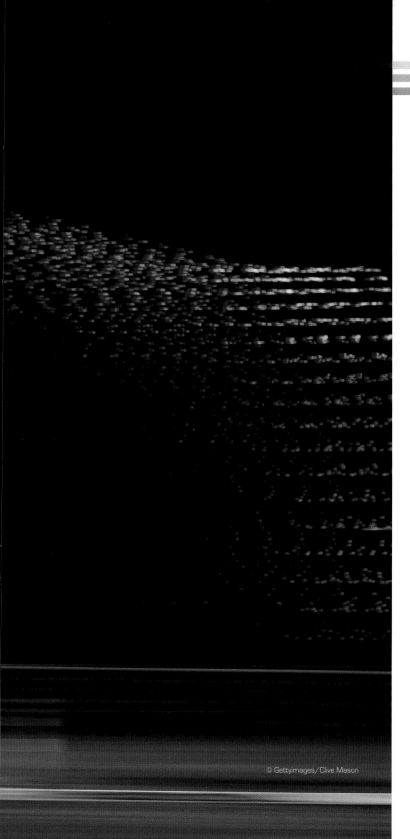

2010

SUCCESS COMES WITH THE FINAL SPRINT

Before the start of the 2010 season, Vettel had the word "Monza" written on his helmet: perhaps he had a premonition of the glorious thread that would connect the historic Italian racetrack with the one in Abu Dhabi. On 14 September 2008 Sebastian had driven in Toro Rosso's first victory, as well as – at the age of 21 and 74 days – becoming the youngest Grand Prix winner ever. A little more than two years later, on 14 November 2010, he brought Red Bull the first world title of its relatively short life. Aged 23 and 134 days, Sebastian also beat Lewis Hamilton's record, becoming the youngest F1 world champion ever.

On the eve of the last race of the season, such a goal seemed almost impossible: Ferrari's Fernando Alonso was leading with 246 points, while Sebastian's team mate, Mark Webber, was second with 238. Vettel, who had scored 231 points was only third: considering that reaching the Spanish driver meant filling a 15-point gap, the only way for him to win the world title was to win the final race and hope that none of his direct rivals shared the podium with him.

The 2010 overall ranking reflected the weird pattern of the season. At the beginning, BrawnGP (which had been acquired by Mercedes and hired evergreen Michael Schumacher) seemed to have lost

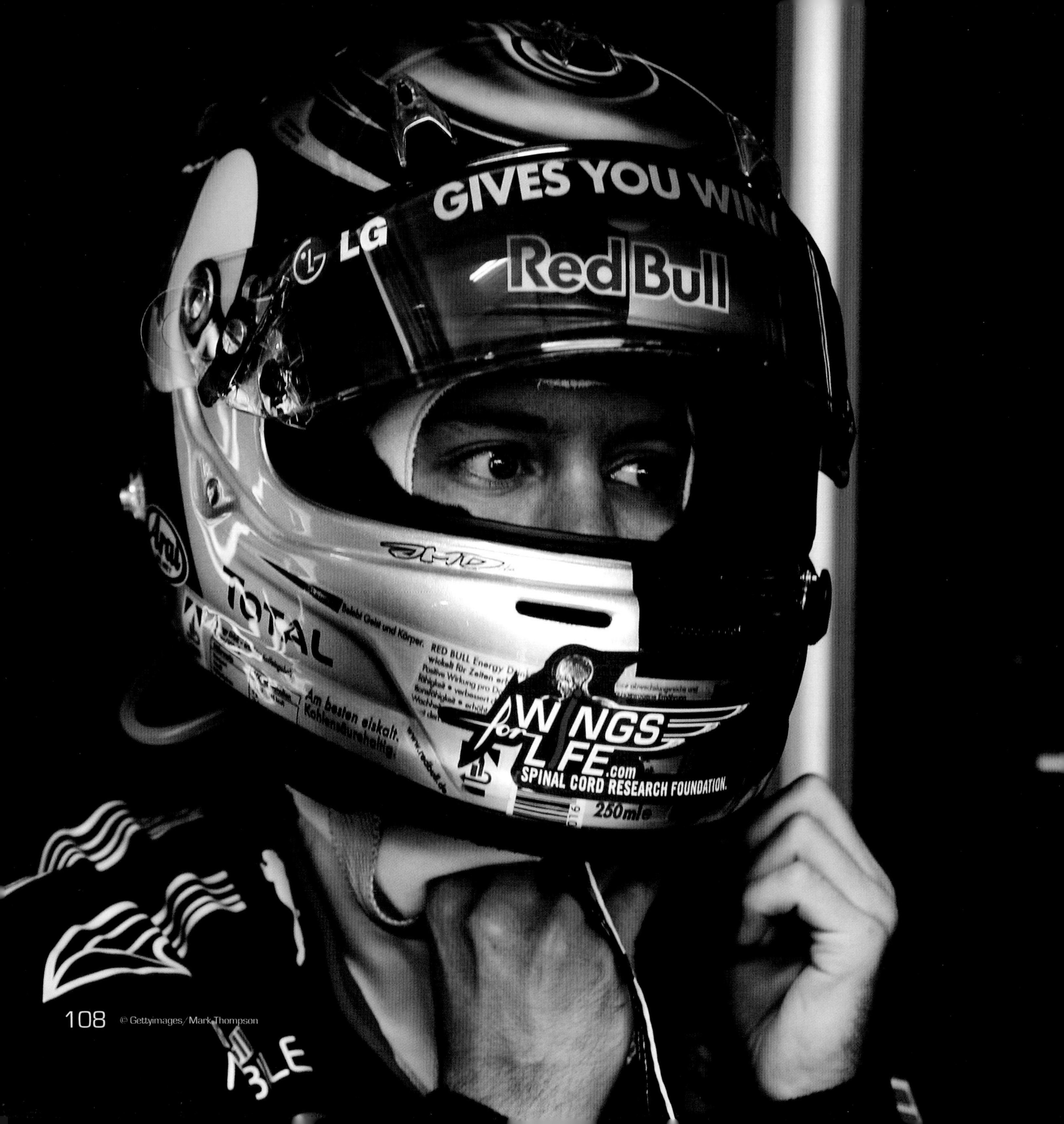

 © Gettyimages/Mark Thompson

the competitive advantage that the double diffuser had provided in 2009, and the single-seats that Adrian Newey had designed for Red Bull performed better than the other cars. However, the team found it hard to take advantage of such supremacy during the course of the year; this was due to the cars' fragility, and the many mistakes made by both the pit crew and the drivers. As for Vettel, he had won pole position in qualifying for the first race. However, during the official competition he was forced to slow down because of a loss of power after problems with a spark plug: in the end he came fourth. Something similar happened during the following Australian Grand Prix: a screw nut in the brake camber loosened while he was leading the race and he was forced to retire.

Sebastian Vettel poses in front of the "Wings for Life" logo. Since May 2010, Vettel and his team mate Mark Webber are ambassadors of this not-for-profit foundation, which supports scientific and clinical research against spinal cord injuries. In this picture, they both pose with Heinz Kinigadner, motocross World Champion in 1984 and 1985.

Sebastian's performances were quite uneven: during the season, his three victories (Malaysia, Valencia, Japan) and five podiums (Monaco and Singapore, second place; Spain, Germany and Hungary, third place) co-existed with lacklustre performances (China, Canada, Great Britain) and two crushing failures. The first one happened in Turkey, with a little help from Webber: during the 40th lap Sebastian tried to overtake his team mate at bend 12; in reaction, Mark bumped into him, handing McLaren the chance of a double podium on a plate. While getting out of his

damaged RB6, Seb beat his index finger on the temple: "that guy's completely mad". But it wasn't all Webber's fault: Vettel had certainly contributed to causing the accident as well. Peace needed to be restored within the team, and Helmut Marko and Christian Horner worked very hard to re-establish it after that race.

The second accident took place in Spa, in a Belgian GP characterised by difficult weather conditions. While trying to overtake Button on the 17th lap, Vettel went off his racing line, ending up in a water puddle, he then lost control of his car, which crashed into the McLaren. Jenson retired from the race, while Sebastian continued driving: his behaviour was punished with a drive-through penalty, which made him lose ground and he finished 15th in the end.

Munich: Mark Webber and Sebastian Vettel lead the Monaco GP, at the end of which Vettel will come second behind his team mate.

Vettel races in the rain in the ill-fated Belgian GP. His collision with Jenson Button's McLaren will cost him many precious points at the end of the race.

2010: on the eve of the German GP, Sebastian Vettel drives on the streets of his home town, Heppenheim. In the town's square, the town's idol signs autographs for his fans.

Hockenheim: Sebastian sits in his RB6 during qualifying for the German GP. Despite starting from the first row, he will surrender to Alonso and Massa's Ferraris and finishes in a disappointing third place.

114   © Gettyimages/Vladimir Rys

Christian Horner and Sebastian Vettel ironically present a baby walker to Bernie Ecclestone for his 80th birthday on the same day as the Korean GP.

Monza, 2010: Sebastian Vettel attends the press conference for this biography's first edition, the book lies on the table in front of him.

His hopes of winning the title seemed to vanish completely in Korea: his Red Bull's engine burned out nine laps before the end while he was leading the race. However, after recovering from the disappointment, the German driver proved that both he and Red Bull still believed in victory. Two weeks later in Brazil Vettel was leading the race, followed by Webber, whose overall score was much closer to Alonso's at that time. Everyone thought that Red Bull would soon order Sebastian to slow down and let his team-mate take his place but it didn't happen. It looked like a self-destructive choice...but Vettel started in pole position in Abu Dhabi, ahead of Webber, who started in sixth place. Alonso was in third, behind Hamilton: Ferrari seemed to have already tasted victory...but Alonso had a bad start, and was immediately overtaken by Button; later on, during the 19th lap, he was summoned back to the pits to "cover" Webber, who had had his pit-stop three laps earlier. This undermined Fernando's race: when he finally got back on the track he was still running ahead of Mark but he was also behind Vitaly Petrov's Renault, and stayed behind Petrov until the finishing line. Alonso came seventh, right before Webber. Vettel had sped off from pole position like a bat out of hell: in the end he won the race, reached the top of the world rankings for the first time in the season, and leapt with joy. For it wasn't just the first time: it was also the most important one.

Vettel celebrates his victory in Interlagos, establishing himself as a credible candidate for the world title. A frowning Mark Webber stands on the second step of the podium on his right, on his left are Christian Horner and Alonso, who was third in the race.

Scenes from a miracle: after his success in Abu Dhabi, an exhausted Vettel poses between Helmut Marko, Adrian Newey and Christian Horner. He is now officially the 2011 world champion.

THE LEADER OF THE SEASON

Sebastian Vettel made his mark in the history of F1 thanks to a year where his talent was rewarded. His statistics for 2011 are self-explanatory: 11 victories, 15 pole positions (a record for one season) and 392 points – 122 more than Jenson Button, runner-up at the end of the season. It's as if the gap between them amounted to 4.88 whole races! Vettel was the last world champion of the Bridgestone era, and he is also the first winner of the Pirelli era.

Although such a fact might seem trivial, it is in reality one of the crucial factors that explain why the German driver dominated the last F1 season. Because of Sebastian's great potential, or perhaps due to the quality of the car that Adrian Newey designed for him, Sebastian figured out very quickly how to optimise the use of the Pirelli tyres. Such skilfulness had struck the Italian technicians already during the winter, despite the fact that compared to their competitors, Red Bull still hadn't delivered outstanding times. Speed, dependability and technical perfection were the cornerstones of a season during which Sebastian stood out as undisputed leader right from the start

Sebastian Vettel, the 2011 season's
true hero bursts out laughing.

(while the previous year he had reached the top of the rankings in the very last race); his team mate Mark Webber – who had brilliantly proved to be a match for him during the previous season – proved to be no competition.

Although Red Bull was unbeatable during the qualifying sessions, its cars didn't compete as clearly as the previous year in the races. However, they never broke down and that was enough to generate an incredible winning streak. At the beginning of the season, Sebastian won six races out of nine (Australia, Malaysia, Turkey, Spain, Monaco, Valencia); in China he came second, but only because of the team's decision to let him make one less pit stop than his rivals, which forced him to slow down during the last few laps. The second place he obtained in Canada was due to one of the very few mistakes he made during the whole season (during the third last lap Button was hot on his heels and he spun around), while in Great Britain he had to give in to Fernando Alonso - who demonstrated, for once, a superior strategy and a better pace.

Before the beginning of the summer break, the world rankings showed that his competitors had started gaining ground: Vettel delivered his worst performance of the season right in his "home race" in which he came

Suzuka, 9 October: thanks to his third position in the Japanese GP Vettel leads the world championship.

fourth. However, when racing restarted after the break, the Red Bull cars were able to call the shots even on the two racetracks on which they were supposed to encounter the most difficulty– that is to say, Spa and Monza. After these victories, guessing who would win the world title became rather easy. The obvious answer to such a question emerged in Suzuka, on 9 October, after another masterly victory in Singapore. In Japan Vettel started third on the grid, behind Button (the only other driver who could still win the title) and Alonso. He became, at the age of 24 and three months, the youngest driver to ever win the F1 world title twice. He had achieved more than his idol, Schumacher, and Alonso himself. "This has been an amazing season" –

he declared, right after the race – "Our secret is not actually the quality of our cars, but the continuity of our results and the solidity of our team".

Vettel's winning streak resumed in Korea, when he brought Red Bull the Teams championship, also thanks to Webber's third place. He then dominated the debut Indian GP, took his fourteenth pole position in Abu Dhabi, equaling a record for the season set by Williams Renault's Nigel Mansell 19 years before. "Had I been told this at the beginning of the season, I wouldn't have believed it", said Vettel, shortly before revealing that the English driver had written to him after the race in India. "I felt more moved than when I equalled the record. I had only seen Nigel at London's waxworks museum before!". But fate played one of its tricks during the official race: despite sprinting away immediately after the starting signal, Sebastian suffered a puncture that forced him to quit the race after only 500 metres. His disappointment was so striking that even Bernie Ecclestone rushed to the pit-lane to comfort him.

At the last race of the season, in Interlagos, he achieved another important goal: with his fifteenth pole position he finally broke Nigel Mansell's world record. During the race, however, a problem with the gears forced him to slow down, allowing his team mate to overtake him and gain his first victory of the season. Vettel came second: nothing to complain about, he admitted, after such a year...

Vettel's Red Bull built by Adrian Newey
dominates the 2011 season. In Japan, Vettel stands
on the podium holding his trophy.

Suzuka: The Red Bull crew celebrate Sebastian Vettel, once again Formula One's champion.

© Gettyimages/Clive Mason

© Gettyimages/Clive Rose

Suzuka by night: a few memories of Vettel's celebrations after his second world title.

126

© Gettyimages / Mark Thompson

© Gettyimages / Mark Thompson

*Korea, 16 October:
the team cheers
for Vettel and Webber
who have brought
Red Bull the leadership
in the team ranking.*

© Gettyimages / Clive Rose

Sebastian Vettel looks up to the sky, dedicating his victory to Marco Simoncelli (whom he had met while promoting a campaign for road safety) and Dan Wheldon. Simoncelli died during a MotoGP race in Malaysia, while Wheldon was killed during an IndyCar race in Las Vegas.

Sebastian drinks champagne from the cup he won after dominating the Indian GP. He started from pole position and also ran the fastest lap during the race.

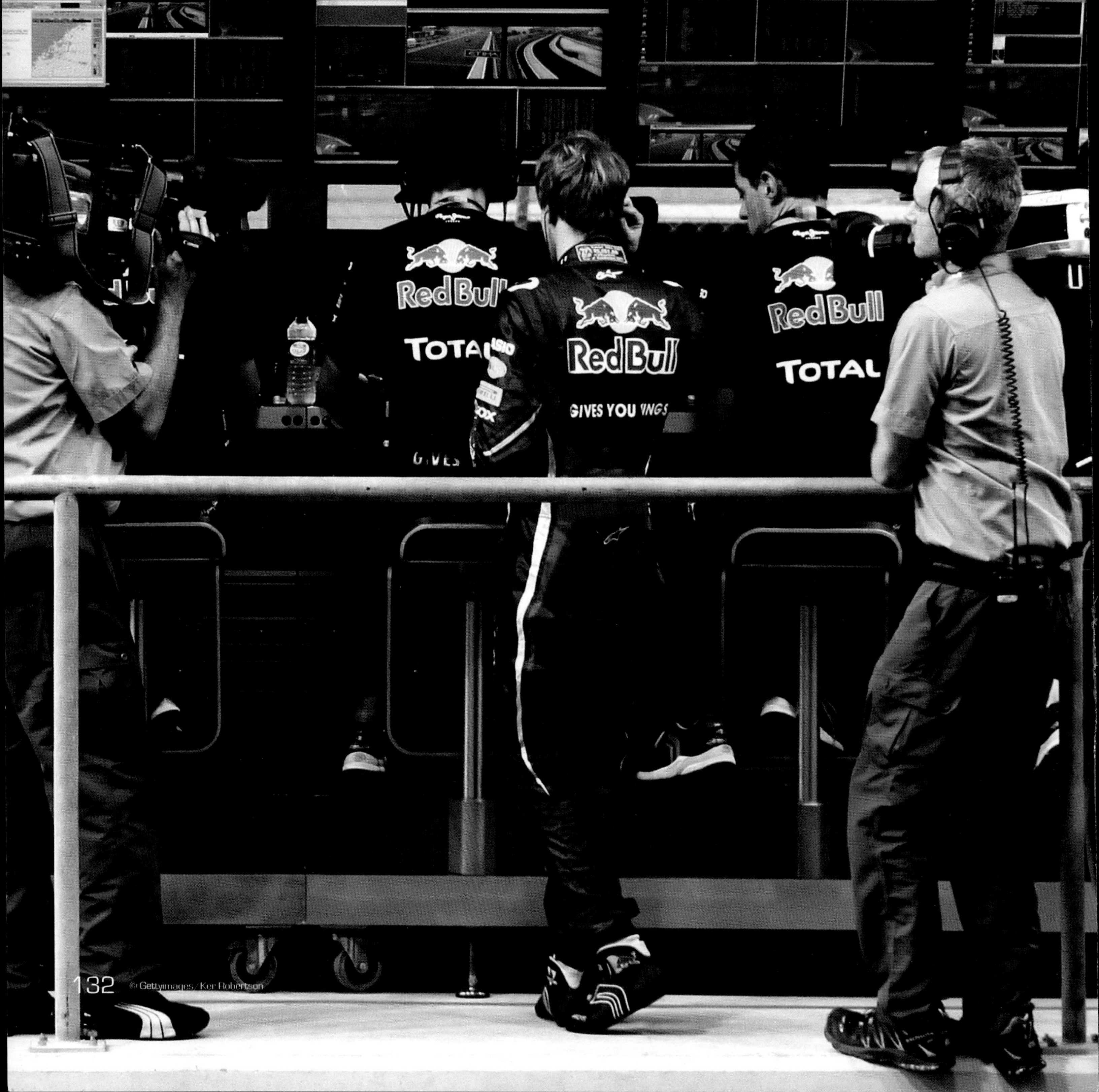
Red Bull
TOTAL
Red Bull
GIVES YOU WINGS
Red Bull
TOTAL

*Abu Dhabi: Sebastian Vettel watches the GP
in the pit-lane after being forced to retire only 500 metres
from the starting line due to a puncture.*

*The German driver, holder of two World Titles,
set his fifteenth pole position during qualifying
in Abu Dhabi, breaking the world record of 14 pole
positions in a season that Nigel Mansell set in 1992.
As a matter of fact, the moustache Sebastian
is wearing to celebrate resembles the one
sported by the English driver.*

End of the season in Interlagos: the whole Red Bull team celebrates Webber and Vettel's success on the podium. It's the end of an incredible year, marked by 12 victories and the top two places in the final race.

135

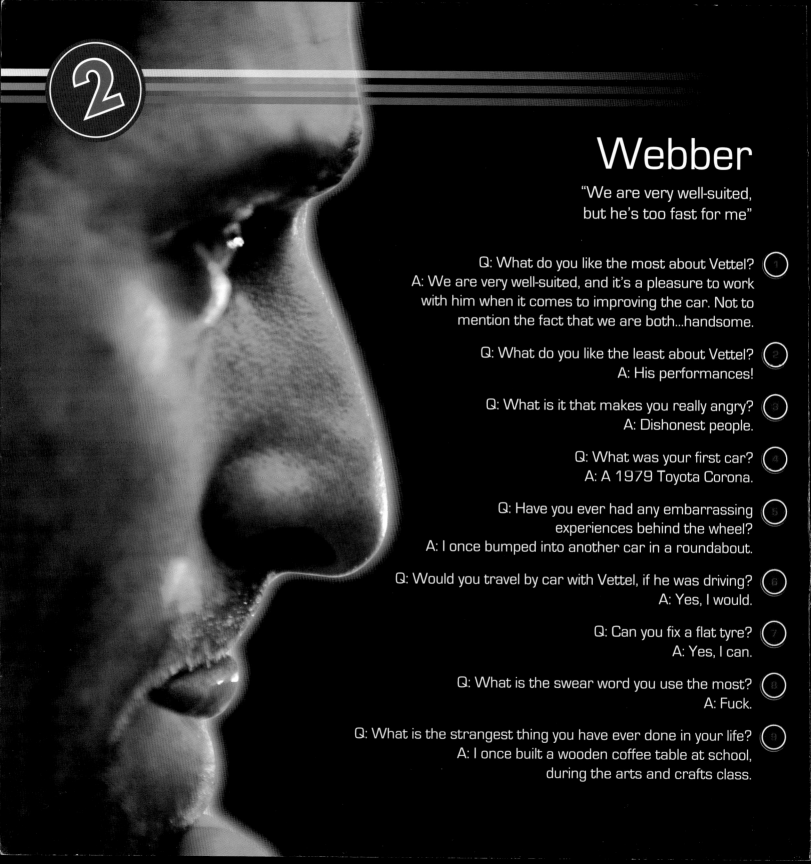

Webber

"We are very well-suited,
but he's too fast for me"

Q: What do you like the most about Vettel? ①
A: We are very well-suited, and it's a pleasure to work with him when it comes to improving the car. Not to mention the fact that we are both...handsome.

Q: What do you like the least about Vettel? ②
A: His performances!

Q: What is it that makes you really angry? ③
A: Dishonest people.

Q: What was your first car? ④
A: A 1979 Toyota Corona.

Q: Have you ever had any embarrassing ⑤
experiences behind the wheel?
A: I once bumped into another car in a roundabout.

Q: Would you travel by car with Vettel, if he was driving? ⑥
A: Yes, I would.

Q: Can you fix a flat tyre? ⑦
A: Yes, I can.

Q: What is the swear word you use the most? ⑧
A: Fuck.

Q: What is the strangest thing you have ever done in your life? ⑨
A: I once built a wooden coffee table at school, during the arts and crafts class.

Vettel

"Mark is very funny, and there's
no mistaking his Australian accent!""

1   Q: What do you like the most about Webber?
A: His strong sense of humour.

2   Q: What do you like the least about Webber?
A: Sometimes I cannot understand his Australian accent.

3   Q: What is it that makes you really angry?
A: Tailbacks and traffic.

4   Q: What was your first car?
A: As BMW ambassador, I had a M3.

5   Q: Have you ever had any embarrassing
experiences behind the wheel?
A: Not really. I had troublesome experiences, like everyone,
but I always managed to escape unharmed.
When I'm not on a racetrack, I drive very carefully.

6   Q: Would you travel by car with Webber, if he was driving?
A: Why not? I would, even if he's a bit crazy.

7   Q: Can you fix a flat tyre?
A: Yes, but it's much easier to call road service.

8   Q: What is the swear word you use the most?
A: Scheiße, like a good German.

9   Q: What is the strangest thing you have ever
done in your life?
A: I tried a parachute jump in 2007.

Q: What is your most recurring dream?
A: Uhm...what is the next question?

Q: If you had to star in a film,
which part would you like to play?
A: An undercover spy.

Q: Can you cook?
A: No, I can't.

Q: Who would you like to invite for dinner?
A: Muhammad Ali.

Q: What is the first thing
you notice in a woman?
A: Her eyes.

Q: What is the most expensive gift you
ever offered someone?
A: The telephone I have in my car.

Q: On the human side, who is the driver
you like the most?
A: Rubens Barrichello.

Q: And the most unpleasant one?
A: Next question, please.

Q: What makes you really proud?
A: The family I grew up in.

Q: Are you superstitious?
A: Not at all.

Q: What do you focus on while you're driving?
A: I concentrate on improving myself.

10 Q: What is your most recurring dream?
A: Becoming world champion.

11 Q: If you had to star in a film,
which part would you like to play?
A: I would be the director.

12 Q: Can you cook?
A: I can prepare simple dishes, such as pasta.

13 Q: Who would you like to invite for dinner?
A: No one in particular: just my family,
and a couple of friends.

14 Q: What is the first thing you notice in a woman?
A: Her eyes, of course!

15 Q: What is the most expensive gift
you ever offered someone?
A: I can't remember, but the price of a gift is not important
to me. What matters most is the thought behind it.

16 Q: On the human side, who is the driver you like the most?
A: Kimi Raikkonen.

17 Q: And the most unpleasant one?
A: Kimi, again.

18 Q: What makes you really proud?
A: Winning a race, defeating all my opponents.

19 Q: Are you superstitious?
A: Yes, I am.

20 Q: What do you focus on while you're driving?
A: I concentrate on the task I'm performing.

SEBASTIAN VETTEL

Born in Heppenheim on 3/7/1987
Star sign: Cancer
Height: 174 cm.
Weight: 64 kg.
Education: German secondary school leaving qualification

CAREER
Before F1 (2001-2006)

2001	Winner of the kart European Junior Championship.
	Winner of the kart German Junior Championship.
	Winner of the Junior Monaco Kart Cup.
	Winner of the Paris-Bercy kart race.
2002	6th place in the European ICA Senior Championship.
2003	2nd place in the German Formula BMW – ADAC Championship.
	Recognised as best debutant of the year, thanks to his 5 victories.
2004	Winner of the German Formula BMW – ADAC Championship (18 victories).
2005	5th place in the Formula 3 Euroseries Championship.
	Recognised as debutant of the year, thanks to his 6 places on the podium.
2006	2nd place in the Formula 3 Euroseries Championship (3 victories).
	2 victories in the Renault World-Series Championship.

FORMULA ONE

2005	First test session with BMW Williams.
2006/07	Test driver with BMW Sauber.
2007	1 race with BMW Sauber (1 point in the world championship).
	7 GPs with Toro Rosso, and 14th place in the world championship.
2008	A season with Toro Rosso: first pole position, first victory (in Monza)
	and 8th place in the world championship.
2009	A season with Red Bull Racing: 4 pole positions, 4 victories, 2nd place in the world championship.
2010	Red Bull Racing, 10 pole position, 5 victories, World Champion
2011	Red Bull Racing, 15 pole position, 11 victories, World Champion

CAREER TOTAL
Sebastian Vettel
has taken part in 81 GPs:

21   victories
30   pole positions
9   fastest lap awards
A total of 773 points

Originally published by EditVallardi 2010 under the title Sebastian Vettel:
La storia e la carriera del più giovane vincitore di un Gran Premio di Formula Uno

Italian edition © by EditVallardi 2011
English translation © Souvenir Press Ltd 2011

First published in Great Britain in 2012 by Souvenir Press Ltd
43 Great Russell Street, London WC1B 3PD

ISBN 9780285640856

Authors: **Andrea Cremonesi and Marco Degl'Innocenti**

Translation by: **Federica Silvi**

Graphics co-ordinator: **Diego Galbiati**

Editorial co-ordinator: **Cecilia Vallardi**

Photographs provided by **Getty Images, GEPA Pictures,**
Red Bull Photofiles/Damiano Levati, BMW Motorsport,
the archives of Gerhard Noack – GN Motorsport, Mirco Lazzari,
Angelo Scaroni, the archives of EditVallardi and the archives of 'Gazzetta dello Sport'.

The photos of Trofeo Bandini (Brisighella 2009) have been provided by **Foto Express.**

Many thanks to Norbert Vettel, Britta Roeske, Bettina Pieri, Gerhard Noack,
Britta Heck, Francesco Assirelli, Fabiana Valenti.

Special thanks to Ercole Colombo and Alberto Crippa.

Printed December 2011